That Place
Where You Opened
Your Hands

University of Massachusetts Press

AMHERST AND BOSTON

That Place Where You Opened Your Hands

Susan
Leslie
Moore

ISBN 978-1-62534-510-3 (paper)

Designed by Deste Roosa
Set in Garamond Premier Pro
Printed and bound by Maple Press, Inc.

Cover design by Milenda Nan Ok Lee
Cover art by Emily Winfield Martin, *Portrait of Evaline,* © 2019. Courtesy of the artist.

Library of Congress Cataloging-in-Publication Data
Names: Moore, Susan Leslie, author.
Title: That place where you opened your hands / Susan Leslie Moore.
Description: Amherst : University of Massachusetts Press, [2020]
Identifiers: LCCN 2019044558 | ISBN 9781625345103 (paperback) | ISBN
    9781613767580 (ebook) | ISBN 9781613767597 (ebook)
Subjects: LCGFT: Poetry.
Classification: LCC PS3613.O5684 T47 2020 | DDC 811/.6—dc23
LC record available at https://lccn.loc.gov/2019044558

British Library Cataloguing-in-Publication Data
A catalog record for this book is available from the British Library

for Phil Ottum, for all that you are
for Laura Kate and Max Denning, my bright lights

CONTENTS

IV

That Place
Where You Opened
Your Hands

I

BEGINNING

I was born, maybe. Maybe I was torn
from a cloud and a bird set me down
on the ground. Maybe I miss the sky.
Maybe my mother's violin was the music
that led me to her. Maybe I first appeared
in a palm tree or the dust on an Iowa farm.
Maybe I grew up out of the earth, a bulb
someone shoved in the dirt and forgot
until I emerged. Maybe I learned the word
mother like a wish scribbled on the back
of a matchbook, like a hymn we never get right.
Convince me I wasn't made from an orange
squeezed over a petri dish or pulled from the sand
of a California beach. My ancestors gazed at the sky
and plucked me from the atmosphere. They sang
hymns about heaven and farming. The hymns
I like best are the ones where we get to walk
with Jesus in the garden. He tells me I am
his own and then he disappears. Remind me
how I landed here, how my mouth and fingers
look like your mouth and fingers. Remind me
I'm an animal inside a ghost of those who came
before me, and the sound a violin makes
is the sound of the sun in bloom, and whenever
I think I've had enough of the sky it changes,
the clouds shift into a pattern that looks
like a parade of giant baby heads or a carpet
of floating whales, and if I could lift my voice
to the rafters, if I could float beyond the trees,
maybe I'd remember why I came.

INSIDE OUR HOUSE IS ANOTHER HOUSE

where everything we say to each other
flies around the walls and fireplace before
coming quietly to rest on top of our heads.

Above our roof is another roof, where birds
organize the sky. Laying aside all our
stored up hurts we slip into bed

and burrow to the center of the mattress
where someone has built a small theme park.
If I shrink myself fast enough I can ride

the Ferris wheel before dark. If I leave a
trail of popcorn the tiny lions will escape
from their cages. We string lights around

the ceiling beams and lean out the bedroom
window to see if the wind is strong
enough for kites. With the right knife

and string I could build one from
a broken chair and ferns. In some situations
you might find me amazing—or more

than a little ordinary. What if I filled
the bathtub with water and let it overflow
until all the furniture floated? Then we could

swim through the house and decide
what to save. What would you
think of me then?

dissolved if we stared long enough. You said unless
we were full of each other we'd only be cardboard
cutouts in a sky that continues whether or not
we were there to witness. Whether we were part
of the landscape or only passing through.
I had a good time today thinking about Jesus.
Everyone gets murdered eventually and only
the lucky ones get to choose the weapon that
will be their undoing. I wanted to flatten
the mountains so they'd fit more neatly
against the sky. You were outside pushing
your feelings into clouds. I'm doing pretty well
with this incarnation—less settled and the seasons
come at me harder. I left all the lights on and then
walked through the house and turned them off,
stopping at each window to look for a face pressed
against the glass. I wanted to die standing up,
looking toward the horizon at something moving
toward me, a ship or a really big animal. You said
unless we rubbed our bodies together we wouldn't
understand beauty. I wanted to hold my skull
in my hands, to know how the bones fit together
and the place I could press on hard to make it shatter.

Tell her wait, little interrupter. Why bother
she is slow. She is field hungry, moving
to the edge of the garden, where she wants
to stay and stay. Spring on its way, why listen?
She is solidly hers. Ducks overhead and the sky
a speckled target. A suggestion of owls in the trees.
The trees repeat her name. How the trees insist.
The birdbath unfreezes, the ground sprouts
and shifts. Tell her back to the house with its curtains
and floors. Tell her dress the paper dolls in leaves,
give them paper knives and forks. Stand them on the counter.
Tell her lovely, little negotiator. She would rather gather
mice. She has had it with the roses. How the bugs persist.
Tell her she can wish for goats eating up the weeds—
she can hope for rabbits. Deer lingering by the fence.
She wants her animals near. She wants the only sound
to be their movements. Call her steady. Tell her resist.

SUBURB

Small sigh of pleasure,
where is my leisure.

The problem of the lawn.

Every bird at the feeder
the same size, the same
shade of brown.

The sky holds clouds
and escaping trees.

In between,
the problem of the lawn.

Planes carry passengers
who wonder
who will take them home
once they land.

I want to dig under the foundations
of every house on my block.
I want to see what the dirt
looked like before people arrived.

My children ride their bikes
in front of the house.
They whisper
about money they find
on top of my dresser.
They think I don't know
they steal from me.

Let the mourning doves
that gather on the sidewalk
fly away and return
with messages folded in their beaks.

Messages I can keep.

TO TAKE

I stole another woman's only scarf
and fed the calf and brushed its coat.
I tore the scarf to pieces and swore
I'd never leave the lake. The map of the lake
had a place marked by an arrow.
I buried the scarf there. I lived a little too close
to the shore and the pelicans gathered at
my back door. I emptied a bucket of fish
in the kitchen sink and opened the window wide.
Will you believe me when I said I didn't mean
to steal it? The scarf was hers, and no one there
to tell me not to take it. The pelicans
dived toward the window, but only one
made it in. The smallest one. Do you know
what happened then—how it filled its bill
with fish and flew back out the way
it came? The fish a gift for a bird that could
find enough to eat without me. The scarf
in pieces, buried near the lake with
other secrets kept nearby. I slept while the frogs
and flies sang back and forth their nighttime
songs. The lake was mine, the calf and pelican
safe in my keeping. I could knit another
scarf and leave it on her doorstep. I could
fill the sink with fish again. I was patient.
It was an accident, the way I took the scarf
when no one stood nearby.

and in the evenings look
for weather. She was field shy,
house hidden, but when she wandered
wondered why the barn & what the roof
meant. The knives all pointed
in the same direction. The geese
arranged like a map. The knives
revealed what she required: a clearing,
a corner, a place to conserve. The heron
a hearing she couldn't get used to.
Knives safe in their drawers
& the weather shifted. The knives
foretold it—said see how
the field. See how it serves.

FROM THE START

If I can't be blameless, let me be superior
in my mistakes. If I can't be singular
in purpose, let me be quietly adrift.
Make me adored and clothed in pinecones.
Make me treed. Let me eat by recipe,
love by touch. Let me direct the forest fire
so it misses the front porch completely.
Give me a way to see past Thursday.
Give me a fishing pole and a tambourine.
If I can't be beautiful, let me be quick.
Show me where the deer wander
when the bats come out. Give me
an owl in the tent at midnight,
a crow in the basement at dawn.
Let me sing on the roof when
the planes depart. Let the planes carry
my song to the water. If I can't be downtown,
give me a museum. Give me a still life
with lemons and a dead bird.
Give me a Cornell box and a rare photograph
of a Parisian street before the war.
Find me a docent with a story to tell.
A forgery replaced by a fake
replaced by the real thing.
Let me lie down with a guitar
and a bird cage. Make me green
and well considered. If I can't be
unraveled, let me be tucked in.

I SAY TO THE STARS GET INSIDE ME

because that's the way I talk to the sky.
Stars are like dead people that can't say goodbye.

Falling in love is so ordinary but if you pushed me
down on the floor I might start to sing.

Go to sleep wake up go to sleep—I need a new
routine. You said unless we are full of
each other our bodies are only machines.

When the world doesn't work I pry it open
with a crowbar and catch everything that falls.

When you won't talk to me I light a candle in my lungs.
I sneak up on starlings to practice strangulation.

Cover my eyes with your hands and I'll pretend
I can't see where your body ends.

I HAVE TRIED HARD TO HAVE APPROPRIATE FEELINGS

I have folded them away like sweaters.
Kept my distance from the moon, visited the sick.

I am proud of the life in my head. Nobody knows
the garden I've seen. I am tender with the suburb.

Some days even the ceiling worries me, the way
it keeps the roof on.

I only cry when the polar bears get to me.
The ones stranded on the melting ice.

Otherwise I'm kept in line by the steady curve
of my driveway, the tight fists of the roses. I can easily converse
about the sweet peas and our eventual disintegration.

The sky has more to say to me than I could
ever hear, given the restricted space between
houses. Frogs sing at night and the whine of the train.

II

mine mine mine mine mine
again with lemons
and a small rabbit
again by the tree
because nowhere else

    back into the picture

    mine the rabbit mine
    the lemon mine his hands

the letters arrive
the children sleep
    sliced dreams
    all day spent looking
        in the garden
          lamb's ear
          foxglove
            lemon verbena
            lemon grass
            lemon balm

June 10th

By the time I got back from the market the walls were singing. The children had been put to bed their cheeks sullen their limbs ecstatic and I was alone with the hare, so used to itself so safe in its body.

and me with my hands in flames.

. . .

17

I didn't write oh into the letter I wrote *o o o*

swell of breath fish's mouth   gathering of suns
the painting without lines   the body without

—thank you for the rabbit

        red flowers grow
        against the wall
        summer continues

Black Rabbit and Lemon (detail), *1864*

The rabbit won't stay in the painting
        the lemon curves

This painting is from the later period. The tablecloth is in disarray. the light slides off the lemons. the shadows recede along a grid. The grid is space. What else is yellow, consider your answer carefully—

where did she get all those canvases?

how did he find his way into her bed?

did she invite him?
she invited him.

the palette was hers entirely.
it shifted over time.

what else is yellow

a newborn   cake batter   pears
hair ribbons   cornflower   daylilies

a woman stands in the kitchen and says what else what else

. . .

Two houses. Both with red roofs. One house is larger. Between the houses, a tree. Behind the houses, a grove of lemons. past the grove, an open field. In front of the houses, an overloved neglected garden. Somewhere underground, a rabbit den.

the dining room and its furniture was created
to suggest ritual
to suggest having enough to eat

> white tablecloths
> cleaning and ironing
> damask and linen

the first day of the month, upon waking she says *rabbit rabbit*—
for luck.

July 19th

For a long time I've been dreaming of becoming someone else. The garden has gotten away from me.

you can't see through a thing—you see with it. the back of their necks, when they were babies—I would put my face on it and breathe . . . how ended it made me feel.

and then the call of the colors, the yellow wing and the red petals,
black fur and pink eyes,

me written there—a small inscription—no, I'm painted there—or covered there, I'm in the world, not part of it, there's nothing there that isn't me.

. . .

She has waited too long. You know how that goes. And the rabbit is a poor substitute. All day it eats grass eats mint eats leaves eats through every sentence the garden writes. It eats faster than she can think of him. It sleeps in the garden between the parsley and lavender and soon it will start multiplying and the offspring will grow and graze, graze and grow and some will leave the garden and some will sleep behind the wall and some will end up eaten. The body should be more singular. But since it's not, she should sleep without him and find out why the painting never works, the canvas warps, the colors falter, and the children or the garden or that field out behind the lemon grove that makes her think run makes her think keep running makes her think run until I disappear, the one thing she tries to possess and hold in one fixed spot ends up being another example of her failure, of her body pushed back and diminished. Of the refusal of any form to satisfy her.

And the colors seem to hiss and echo, of the tree that grows between the houses, of the flowers that hide below the tall grass, of the soft flesh of her children's bodies.

yes she was a bride once, married to the marriage bed.

. . .

the hare is solitary	rabbits are gregarious
the hare sleeps on the open ground	rabbits sleep in warrens—they burrow
hares are born with fur and open eyes	rabbits enter the world naked and blind
hares have longer legs	rabbits bring luck
hares are mad	

looking hard.
she loses the green.
she wants to see
with her hands.
she walks into the orchard
a hundred lemons at her feet.

the children shriek on the stairs.
they drown out his voice
then he's gone.

where does the green begin
some mornings she is all angles.

. . .

Do you have a rabbit?
He is a house rabbit.

He was never a house rabbit. He had wild carnation eyes. I carried him into the garden.
How could I have known there were more?

Of course I knew there were more.

His paws smelled like mint. The children carried him into the garden. They let him go.

look up at the houses that fall into shadows
then lie in the grass
that the rabbits inhabit.

Do you have a brilliant eye?
I believed that you believed I believed in beauty
        unraveled
        unstitched
        unnumbered

    that brightens and darkens
    and dips into shadows

then lie in the grass
  look up at the houses.

It moves along the leaves,
  it enters
   the branches. And from red roof

to red roof she watches
  the picture change.
   It's not the horizon she wants—

she wants to see with her body.
  The flowers excuse themselves,
  the grass ends.

. . .

Because this is about description I am asking you to stop. If you want to know what my house looked like from the inside, you are being asked to stop. I will tell you but you never listen. This conversation has occurred before—it has taken place and then it gave it back—but you never listen so you don't remember. But again: the small red house was for painting. There are paint stains on the floors and the window never latched properly and there's nothing improper about that—so it's a stupid word—but the mice would get in and one of them once wandered into purple paint on his feet on his tail and fled into the garden and his tail flashed through the grass. The larger house was for the usual things the making of meals and the rooms for the beds and the library and the sitting room and the dining room and the stairs that led up to the children's rooms and the room at the back where visitors slept and everything was divided up and yes I hung curtains in the kitchen and yes the maid scrubbed the floor and you accused me of being one who has a maid but I had the money and that's what I spent it on. But then the children got older and I was tired of going back and forth to the little red house and so I started sleeping there.

I don't understand your need for order. Every room in my house had a corner or four. Dust would get under the beds and sometimes I swept it and sometimes she swept it and sometimes it just gathered more dust. Dust is mostly flesh.

. . .

what are you thinking?
I never think anymore.

what are you looking for when you squint into the distance?
     new surfaces.
     a feeling I'm being replaced.

     look closer
     get on your knees
     reach your hands a little farther
          what do you think you'll see?

if all you ever do is what you're asked to do then you will never need to answer when someone asks—what are you up to?

. . .

Red House (detail), *1866*

In the corner is a long disputed corner in the corner of the painting. There are questions about the painter who painted the painting. Most critics believe the painting was painted by a woman and so of course it was her painting some people believe the best way to approach a painting is

to describe the brushstrokes or they use words like abbreviated or high planes of color or they comment on the content or they say astonishingly abstract brushstrokes or they say how were the brushstrokes arranged they say rapid broken brushstrokes but she painted this mostly in reds and yellows and all those primary—by which I mean first—

colors, but in the corner is a small bit of purple and the stroke of the
brush changes.
no one knows how long she lived in the house.

I wouldn't call them strokes.

. . .

his hands reminded her of lemons but she had been reminded of that before.

August 18th

I wondered if you thought perhaps I would fall in love with the rabbit. I think you thought it was possible or was it a joke. I don't want him to tame and relax in my house.

I have been rabbited. I have been up for days planning an escape.

Up for a day or two, anyway.

When I first—well. I have no use for any of that, any before and then after or even trying to describe the way my body felt when—no. Because it traps it in a piece that has to begin and end which never made the least bit of sense. Why create a history for anything like that. Why should I always be eventing. And restricting and confining and placing myself somewhere in the picture.

There are other things. These things are mostly joy. Or unhappiness pushed so far that I start to dissolve.

Which is an effect that is hoped for desired and moved toward.

. . .

endings are hard.

beginnings are smoother.

somewhere in the middle is a texture like embroidery or the way something
hardens right
before it bakes completely or the way the brush moves across a canvas in
a way that we call strokes.

somewhere in the middle she started to move
turn
loosen
inflect herself into

out past the windows
out past the field

an outside that was part of her inside
what takes place in the outside
is more than she could replace inside

the notion of being whole—of having a whole self of being
entirely and only one thing

is not realistic

no one lives like that

. . .

Some have argued end with the diary it was what she said it was what she wrote it can never be disputed how can words be disputed, while the mouse in the corner says just watch me try. Others have said but what about the paintings there were certainly more paintings and who did she give them to did anyone pay her she must have had money and people say what happened to her children what kind of mother could she possibly have been if she didn't mention the children more?

You don't mother your children you become your children you inhabit their bodies as long as they'll let you they push you away and they're gone. You put your face on their necks you breathe and are ended. There is nothing there to be narrated.

So she wanted to begin again. That's what she squinted toward.

I don't know how long she lived in the house.

I don't know who he was.

she didn't want to be a story.

and the gaze that invents the world, the gaze of a woman who loves
        and you can't say it like that anymore, you can't say love
                        you're supposed to think in images
                        you're supposed to situate yourself
                        you're supposed to give something back to the reader.
                                for all the time they give you
                                        a sort of contract

    in the house there was dust and children and after the rabbit
                        arrived more rabbits arrived which is what usually
                        happens

                                and happens some more
                                which was probably a joke he was making
                                why he gave her the rabbit I mean

Child with Rabbit (detail of a detail), *1870*

a remarkable example of a space that has been shaped by a feeling
attributed first to another painter until the painting under the painting

was recovered   escaped

September 9th

the red hiss of the grass then can sound like sighing.

WHY IS POETRY WRITTEN IN LINES

> question from a book on prosody

Because a line
is the shortest distance

from language
to that place

where you opened
your hands.

FROM THE NATURALIST'S NOTEBOOK
Division:

Because it splits
and wants to be sectioned,
not bolted or cadavered.
Not fleshed or wasted.

I'm in my underwear,
walking on wet grass.
The morning rubs off on my feet.

Dahlias buried and gone,
they'll never burst
or need staking.
Coreopsis shoved
and tucked away.

What I should have done
was plant according to the guide—
full sun not sometimes. A plan.

I hung a basket off the eaves,
color spilled on all sides.
In summer there is no middle,
no place to draw a line and say half—
here is your half.

I'm inside out in the garden.

BATS

I like the way bats fly toward my hair
at dusk, like I might be that tree they've been
searching for. I'm territory. I had a dream where

someone called *mom mom*, and I sat up in bed
and said *what*. I'm marked. Today I boasted
how well I could wield a kitchen knife

and you knew I was lying as soon as I opened
the drawer. The one with all the knives.
I wonder how it feels to have wings instead of arms,

to exist in two frequencies. Some bats can't feel the sky
without another bat telling them where it is,
but some learn to navigate the space

between buildings alone. I'm tired
of not knowing what comes next which is a bad
way to live. After the after life, what then?

I'm prepared to come back as a mouse
or a mule deer, but don't think I'll be content
with just dirt. I loved sideways, like a train that swerves

right before it collides with another train. I lived
like a Ferris wheel. I like to think of the river
as a series of raincoats flung off by people long

before us. I like to think of you sleeping next to me
like you've always been there. I had a feeling
you would show up today is something I never

get tired of saying. Like feelings could get us
anywhere. If I opened the door onto the balcony,
if I knocked down the wall between my apartment

and my neighbor's, would I be able to walk through?
If I could see by the sound my singing made
when it bounced into people or trees would

that make me a better person? What would I do
with all that awareness? If the river were a swimming pool
how far could I swim before I had to come up for air?

SELF-PORTRAIT AS MATH

Equate me with nothing, I can't be a sign.
Don't solve me for *ex*. Solve me for *why*.

I want to count my bad decisions. I want
to count what can't be numbered. How many

times have I left my old self behind only
to discover her trailing behind me. She knows

me better. She knows my selves diverge
even on a straight line. That person I wanted

to be, baking loaves of bread for all the lost
orphans, armed with a sturdy wisdom—

subtract her. Subtract patience. Add the crows
that call and urge me to follow. Add the shiny

coins I can't stop collecting at every intersection.
I never have enough pockets to hold them.

III

*

Yesterday a God.
Today a refusal.

Yesterday a surface.
Today a delusion.

Yesterday a window.
Today a refusal.

Yesterday a garden.
Today a delusion.

*

Missed my calling, cartography.
Missed my calling, goose girl to the swan.

*

I should have been a cataloger
of something consequential:

      inventions of convenience—
            the ironing board, the flashlight.
      the uses of logic—
            fidelity, systems of defense.

I should have learned to sail.
      (my boat at half-mast rescued & the map under the water)

I should have learned to swim.

*

where it is broken   I mend it
where it is creased   I iron it
where it hungers   I feed it   (berries & the sky is full of holes)

I had to make something
where outside the world—

*

The trees spell my name and my name is a question, is shorthand for limbs and
their leaves are a spell. Their limbs are my branches and a fortune the trees tell.
Their leaves better blankets than letters or limbs.

The hands of the day, and the trees wear my name.

*

Every last sparrow slipped into the sky. Disappeared and the flowers are missing
their bees. I could have crossed oceans. Slept in the forest, woke with my head
full of mice.

Yesterday an owl.
Today some confusion.

*

I haven't dreamed of flying for a while. Heron near the pond and geese geese
geese but stopped to count them only once. Bats at dusk escaping from the trees.

But how I love the tidy surface of a wall that holds the beams in place. A window
with a wide curtain and a sill where dust collects.

Carried the dust in the pockets of my dress. Undressed on the lawn and left the dust in the grass.

Then I would become less useful. Rust like a shovel in the rain.

*

I listed the stars
      in brief constellations
I mapped my position—

Assemblage of hearts and then waiting.

FROM THE NATURALIST'S NOTEBOOK
Propagation:

Gathered lavender. What's planted,
grows. Rip out the roots and what's left

resuscitates or rots.

Nearby, water. Any little thing is water.
Nearby, a memory I had of another time.

My daughter practices her flute
sitting crosslegged in front
of a full-length mirror.
She circles the edge of a note.

I was celebrated in the landscape.
The arborvitae said yes,
the roses, of course.

A fireplace glorified by ferns.
A windowsill heavy with violets—

the house documents my presence.
The house is where.

The beds unmake. The dishes occur.

My children hunt for me
upstairs and down.

EVERY DAY IS A NEW DAY

—like today, a ridiculous day, when the shoes are in my way
and the dog trips me in the hall. They say a dog's
a wolf but I don't believe it, a dog's a wolf like

I'm a peasant in a mud hut. There's a raccoon
in the hedges, sleeping behind the squirrel.
It's not a dream, it's the alternate reality

where we're living with creatures and our time line
is cursed. Or worse. I was first to the fence
with my offerings, I sighed when I should have been

praying. I don't know what I believe anymore
but I still pray, and not a just-in-case prayer or
a foxhole prayer. It's a prayer with a beak and a splintered

wing. There's a deer in my backyard eating grass
and staring at me—mule deer, wolf dog, birds at the feeder.
I'm far from the hut, ripe in the suburbs, and I can't find my keys.

I can't find a clean pair of pants or a pen to sign the permission slips.
Let me help you with that buckle, that zipper, that fistful of shells

we brought back from the beach. They looked better in the sand.

The Canada geese and spent primrose make me feel hopeful
and wronged. I'm reading my future in coffee ground
patterns, reading my life in the dirt and the clouds.

Sun in my eyes and knife on the counter, I'm feeling like
a new day, a blue sky day with a no-bad-news-today
intention, or prayer, whatever, this day.

THE FUCHSIA, THE ORANGE, AND THE DAHLIAS

We were waiting what seemed like a long time,
when someone said they thought the sign
pointing left had been deliberately forged,
and the route to the city had become untenable.
The conversation kept returning to science,
to fields of cows and numbers. Meanwhile
the days paraded their soft perfume. A neighbor
pulled a tapestry from the shelf, and we noticed
how bright the colors were, how the orange
and fuchsia in the bird's wings made it seem
not mythical, but fleeting, and how the dahlias
woven into the garden held a message of purpose,
or the signs of a leisure we couldn't possess.
It was all we could do not to comment on it
for hours. Some of us felt strange in the heat,
as though we could taste the sun in our hair,
or fold it in our hands like paper. The past
was to be shunned—if it knocked, we agreed
not to answer. Such forms of resolve
kept us incorrigible for days.

MARIA

The trees looked like the number seven
and some curves, torn apart by birds.
I graphed it in pencil and left it

by my bed. And so, ambition.
And so, desire. I had a dream that was
mostly arches, and a library where the marble

said, it will always be like this. I sighed with the monks
and sang a married song to the machine
that slept inside me, and when they said,

don't try, you lack, I tried anyway.
The morning was without hands
or windows, so I stitched—underneath

were factored hems and knots and afternoons
unraveling. The roses thorned and tangled,
the least butcher bird called and I answered,

because numbers said yes and to solve means to adore.
My work stole the hours from me and gave
them freshly back and I dug the ground

until the dirt bled my fingers
and at night I made the numbers sing,
I angled the garden until it balanced.

HEDGES

My mother prays for me,
and what I should have done.

People die when the world
stops loving them,
when the world has had enough.

The hedges in our backyard
never grow straight. Neighbor's
fireworks land in our yard.

The hedge can't keep the
weather out, can't keep
my children home when

they need to wander,
when I need to let them.

No one ever left me that I wasn't
glad to see go, even if the scent
of them was everywhere
on my skin and in my clothes.

The scent of lemon and fireflies.
Or once, the scent of bees.

PRAYER

Jesus make me an owl
so I can sleep behind the sun.

Make the forest only mine,
the fir and the alder my hiding.

Where there is thirst,
let me swallow dark pools of mice.

Where there is doubt
fold faith into my wings.

Grant that I may not so much seek
to be understood as to understand

the rabbit's unlucky foot, fastened to the snow.
The broken back of the squirrel.

I DREAMT I WAS YOUR CAT AND THEN THE NIGHT

was not a dream. I thought I was singular,
a wick that wouldn't light. I was a weed

that wouldn't uproot and the dirt
was all the darkness I could live on.

Once I poured everything
I knew about you into a bowl

then turned it upside down
and let it spill. I couldn't contain you.

But only you would know if I stole
the sky and hid it inside me.

I dreamt I ate every bed I'd ever shared.
When you washed the sheets you washed me.

Put me in a bathtub full of milk and I would
drink it all, but only after my thighs turned soft

like the belly of a deer. Then you would know
my body best. If I hid in the drawer like a tablecloth

you could unfold me. Only you would know
if I turned my heart into a door. I dreamt

I caught you in a crawlspace and shined a flashlight
into your mouth to see what your feelings looked like.

EAT OR BE EATEN

Love or be loved.
Lie down with the lambs
and get up with wool.

Take or be taken.
Flee or be fled.

After the rabbit is killed,
and its flesh stripped from
its bones, they chop off its foot.

Soak the foot in Borax,
sew the wound with twine.

Give it to someone else.
Then it brings luck.

HORIZON MEANS A LINE WHERE THE BODY

disappears and is replaced by sky.

I built a nest in your liver.
I left my cells on your sheets.

I know my limbs work best connected
to my body but I like to think of them
as separate animals.

My mouth in charge of my feelings.
My skin a recording of who I used to be.

Calipers measure the distance between
two parts of flesh and then I hand you
a scalpel to rearrange the tissue.

I like to think of you asleep on your back
in a field that reminds you of me—
the way the sky hovers above it.

TO DEFINE: *FETCH*

Certainly a dog fetches.
Most dogs fetch, although
mine never. She lacked
the will to carry.

Servants fetch. Young girls
are fetching if their tights
match their dresses.

But also: an apparition of
a living person. Someone here
but not quite, who haunts the one
who's really here.

Or closer still than that to you—
he won't let go.

You mean the world to him.
His fist closes around your name.

Nature is mature like swan is the past tense
of swim. Like I am hot and cold, a good mother
then a bad soldier, a deserter in a vast desert—
no deserts are small, no dessert is lost on me.
I want cakes lined up on a counter for me, only me,
to swallow whole. Maybe I'm a swan stranded in a room
that looks like a desert only if you have never been
outside. If you have never swum across a lake at the end
of summer with crawfish biting your ankles, if you can't
explain the scar on your wrist, the shudder in your palms
when you try to pray or ask for grace from some upward
facing God, some peasant disguised as knowing, then maybe
you are not like me. Maybe nature made just one and I mature
and celebrate my bad decisions. I'm the natural progression
of a master plan I can't unravel. Put me in a forest
or a high-rise, call me swan or sailboat. Cover me with pearls
and dirt. Let me sleep in an abandoned nest. Let me swim
in an unmapped ocean, no lighthouse visible for miles.

FOR THE NEWLY CINEMATIC

Every so often you want to lie down
and watch the smoke from your cigarette
disappear into the ceiling fan.

It's a short walk from your apartment
to the park downtown. Your backpack
is full of oranges and the tune you hum
is five notes and a little soul, a theme
on all your blurred entanglements.

And the park is full of hissing geese
and strollers. And a couple floats by
in a hot air balloon. The way they drift
makes you feel optimistic, like somewhere
a beautiful guitar waits for you.

You want to lie down and stare at the sky.
When the soundtrack fades there will be
more music. When the people get too
far away you won't try to bring them closer.
You'll start again, with new people.

CLEANING HOUSE WHILE LISTENING TO A TAPE OF ANNE SEXTON

> *But poetry is my love, my postmark, my hands,*
> *my kitchen, my face.*
> —Anne Sexton, letter

There are rooms in this house
where floors are swept and sinks
are scrubbed, rooms where children
sort plastic animals into tribes
and leap from their beds like acrobats.

And there's the room where I undress
and fall into bed with a language
that offers me metaphor, tells me this is that,
and this is like that, if only I could discover
the right way to say it.

Some women marry houses, you said.
I don't completely inhabit this one.

And when I'm sick of poetry
I disappear into this house.
I wash the mirrors and change the sheets.
The winter sun hits the walls and
I turn toward it, warming myself
in its ordinary light.

DOWN AT THE HEELS IN THE DITCH

Give me a snowstorm, get me a hat.
We need weather and boots to walk in,

we need the moon and an unholy din
to keep us in curtains and fish. All that

we want is waterproof fabric and coins
to keep us counting and clutched. Your chin

looks quiverish and sad. Where have you been? We knew
the way but the binoculars burst, the compass was crushed.

The trees can't invent us—they're unsigned and undreamed,
they're cloudstruck and squirreled. The ground is a scene,

a wish. The sky rambles sockless. Give me your gloves
and fetch me a stove, crouch sweetly with me and wonder:

where is the roof of the house we should live in?
what is the name of that bird in your mouth?

I AM CLIMBING INTO BED WITH A STIFF DRINK

and a wildlife identification guide. I am giving up
trying to go it alone. The bird on page twelve
with the spotted wings and red beak hasn't been seen
since the sixties. The yellow rat on the next page eats
endangered beetles that look like rusted buttons.

Some days I'd grow antlers and a tail just to lie at the feet
of an animal and break saltines into its open mouth.
Some days Jesus reaches his hands inside me and squeezes
my lungs until they almost burst with joy—or maybe
it's relief. Then I sleep too long and my feet turn into mice.

What the person lying next to you dreams you can
never really say for sure. Still I want to be known,
like a recipe carried through the years. The black-footed
ferret on page forty-five suffers from habitat destruction.
All its prairie disappeared. I can't feel my ears but I know
they're there, and I can't see much lying in the dark
except the outline of trees against the window. If I squint
they look like the arms of someone trying to break in.

Crack the spine of any animal and you find
leftover parts of birds and fishes. Under my skin
is a network of living things and under that is the real me
is a prayer I like to say. People might wonder some day

what the animal with the long neck was but right now
the giraffe is easy to know. Show someone a photo
in a hundred years and who will recognize me—
my mouth, my neck, that place between my legs.

IV

*

O my mechanical heart,
my wind-up sigh and stutter.
My mistakes, my flower beds.
My resistible sheets, my lazy arms.

O my unwise counsel, my loss.
My wifeness, my echo.

Let the crows argue over the lawn.
Let the dirt sing
its wormed-through song.

My mouth is the freshest vegetable.

*

My mouth is the freshest vegetable.
My cleverness doesn't shimmer.
Doesn't protect. The sky shines
like a photograph of the sky—
flashes of weather and geese.

Crows dive into trees as if
to devour them. Crows
in love with the trees
because trees live in the sky.

Come closer trees. Which
crow would you give up
for me?

*

Which crow would you give up
for me? Which dress would you
lend the sky? A dress to wear
for the rain. The rain marries
the ground and the sky disappears
like a lost nickel. The rain
a music I miss when the rain stops.

To say I want for nothing
would be to lie down in the sky—
to say the sky was mine.

*

To say the sky was mine
and the field envious
and the window gave me
the sky in pieces. To say I never
saw the sky whole—
as though it were possible
to understand the sky.

Geese push against the sky.
The sky enters them and it seems
like progress. The geese the only
weather the sky needs.

The trees would wander
if the dirt let them—
if the dirt didn't love the trees.

*

If the dirt didn't love the trees
the crows would console them.
The crows would sing,
and I would build a home
for the trees and not call it forest.

Call it devotion or what would have been
if the trees didn't own the sky.

Clouds darken and the roofs of houses
all I see from the window. And birds
too fast to name. The birds don't branch—
they wing. To name the birds.

O my mistakes, my flowerbeds.
O my mechanical heart

EVE

I didn't know where I was headed, all I knew was
I wanted to go somewhere. I heard the animals shifting
in their beds of leaves and dirt. I wanted to speak
but no words would follow. The clouds taught me
it's better to listen, my mouth closed like a purse,
my heart shoved behind my throat, where it belonged.
Apples glowed in the trees. There were signs all around me,
if only I could read them. Geese in pairs. Magnolia blossoms
on the ground like discarded dresses of tiny women.
I wanted to fall into sleep like a well, to close my eyes
and wake up changed. I made a guitar from the branches
of a willow and played it near the water's edge. Snakes
vibrated in the grass. I wanted to sing but could only play
my instrument. Apples fell like arrows and I tried to read
their message. To stay or wander farther. To slip into
darkness and sleep like a lamb, or stay awake forever.
I stained my lips with berries, kissed the trees
to leave my mark. No one told me not to.

PRAYER

I want a horse unlovely
and unbridled. I was made

for branch and acorn,
dirt and crow. And if I loved

the trees, was I unseemly
pagan treed? A horse to house

and roam for, the forest doesn't
owl its own. It sparrows.

The trees the same for birdness
as for branch. The horse my forest

I confuse with meadow that
uncomplicates. My unfenced horse

I want for riding. All nights
the same but hands on mane

I was unrested and undone.

OWL AMONG THE RUINS

I am like a desert owl, an owl among the ruins
—Noelle Kocot

I am lonely lost and feathered
lost among the ruins

I am finding it intolerable
to be me but I am excited

for the rain

Once I flew through the desert
welcoming the night

and the statues

sleeping
on their heads

SONNET

She whet her appetite on the lines
of the field. Heron on her doorstep.
The lie that lived inside her, outside the moon
and field. Field where the sheep slept.

Better to open her hands to shyness
than undress with no one in the distance.
No one near. Field lay down with such
precision. Heron fled. Field regretted.

Geese all gathered in their getting.
And how the sky unhinged its netting.
Field from away and trees moved closer

and sheep wandered and she grew smaller.
Or larger, and carried dirt from one piece
of ground to another. And saw the field cease.

LANDSCAPE WITHOUT FIGURES

for Tori

The clouds inhale and all the stars
disperse. When you die, your death

swims around the lake. There should be
a color to paint the sky when someone

forgets your name. There should be
a path of life reserved for the wandering.

Remember me, I said, back when we
were alive? Those were unkempt days.

SIGHT COMES TO OWLS SLOWLY

They leave their nests and their foreheads ache.
They think the day wants to hurt them.

So when I wore my owl suit the atoms of owls
shifted inside me. I climbed into the sky

and they believed me possible owl. I flapped my wings
like night and hidden but I was not so sure

an owl. First I wore the body and then
I wore the head and when I asked for trees

they gave me trees but not how I wanted,
not like limbs to practice dives from sky to bigger sky,

but trees that bent their branches to land me
safely in the sky. Daughter on the ground

but in the sky I rested. When the night was tall
my wings, where trees became more trees and then a sky

to sleep in. A nest and what I found inside cracked shells
and molting. And what I saw was shadows. My sister owls

were far above me. The ground a long way down
and nothing in the trees that heard me.

STILL LIFE, WITH BRICK

> *What does the brick want to be?*
> *It wants to be something greater than it is.*
> —Louis Kahn

What I was after was permanence
and a place to put it. What I was after
refused and bewildered. Sparrows flew
from tree to eave. Darted and hummed.
Let this be a lesson, the way their bodies
carried them so easily to their purpose.

Let this be a lesson—a refrain I returned to
all winter. I was an instrument
in need of tuning. The brick was
emphatic. Full of itself and its endeavors,
it found time to admonish
now look what you've done.

The scientific names for flowers
eluded me. I wanted to know them
intimately, cosmos to columbine,
wren on the lawn. I heard the brick
sigh and settle, and sometimes
it would sing—made of light which has been spent.

I wanted to be used that completely.

ONCE

I was a wife. I folded things—
pieces of paper, socks, feelings.

I was a mother to the smaller
ones. That means I kept their bodies
safe. I wanted to undress the birds,

remove the door hinge from its squeaky frame.
I wanted to protect the landscape—
first the horses, then the mountains
that shone their snow over the field.

I found the only sparrow, left it
by the kitchen window. I shed
so many skins to arrive at your door.

that kept me contained. Change the roof, the gutters,
the bedroom ceiling with glow in the dark stars

in made-up constellations. Change the floorboards
where I hid my sadness. Change the backyard where

we buried the hamster when he died from eating too much
wallpaper. Change the field and the horizon

that lay above it like a mouth that wouldn't open.

Change the trail that led to a clearing where flowers
bent from the weight of their blooms. The blooms

a pattern on a mother's nightgown. The clearing a room
where I wouldn't stay. Change my heart so it beats faster

when the sky opens up to a ladder of geese. My heart
a harvest of longing and rubbed out fingerprints.

Change my hands, my feet, my eyes that couldn't see
the future where another me waited to take my place.

Change the names I gave myself and all the names
I left behind. Change my lungs so they breathe a different air.

TELESCOPE VERSUS MICROSCOPE

All those tiny bugs that crawl along
my eyelids, devouring dead skin.

The edge of space like a hotel room
before your shoes drop in the corner
and your body creases the taut sheets.

The smallest inhalation of breath
when fog moves into the yard.

If I could hover above my life
like an astronaut I might see
how I misunderstood
the shape of it.

A chain of events linked
by repeating attempts to find
a piece of ground that fits.

(SURRENDER)

The bark stacked on the ground
with tracks of insects that bore
into it for food is all that's left of the trees.

I work hard to abandon my former
selves. I climb into them at night
then step out of them each morning.

Giving up the fight is not the same
as letting go and letting go
is more like how an animal leaves
its body only when every part
is extinguished.

When every part of me
is shimmered through
like a river flushed from
its shore. When I give up
what the sky has done to me.

Then the singing begins.

"Diary from the Red House"

    The Red House is an 1873 painting by Camille Pisarro (1830–1903), part of the permanent collection of the Portland Art Museum, Portland, Oregon.

"Bats"

    "The collection of wet known as a river can look like a chain of dark cloth, procession of fat collared and undulating clothes. For some reason I often think of the rivers of the world as a chain of dark slipping coats unbuttoned from continents of bodies and cast into the valleys of the world."
    —Gabriel Gudding, *Literature for Nonhumans*

"The Fuchsia, the Orange, and the Dahlias"

    This poem was inspired by and written for John Ashbery.

"Maria"

    Maria Gaetana Agnesi (1718–99), a mathematician, wrote the first book that discussed both integral and differential calculus. She was also the first woman appointed by a university as a professor of mathematics.

"Cleaning House While Listening to a Tape of Anne Sexton"

    "I can only speak, from my room, my typewriter, to say I was just completing a third book of poems, waiting for someone to produce my play, to either kill it or bring it forth, and am trying myself on a little prose. But poetry is my love, my hands, my kitchen, my face."
    —Anne Sexton, quoted in *Anne Sexton: The Last Summer,* by Arthur Furst

"Owl among the Ruins"

    "I am like a desert owl, an owl among the ruins" is the title of a poem by Noelle Kocott. The words are a variation on a line in Psalm 102.

"Still Life, with Brick"

    Louis Kahn (1901–74) was an American modernist architect.

Cake Train: "Diary from the Red House"
Faultline: "From the Naturalist's Notebook: *Division*"
Hubbub: "Cleaning House While Listening to a Tape of Anne Sexton"
New York Quarterly: "[O my mechanical heart]"
Oregonian: "Down at the Heels in the Ditch"
Perihelion: "To Define: *Fetch*"
Poetry Northwest: "Inside our house is another house"
Rattle: "The Fuchsia, the Orange, and the Dahlias"
Redactions: "Prayer" (p. 43)
Shampoo: "Sight Comes to Owls Slowly"
Tupelo Press Online: "To Take"
Willow Springs: "Bats," "I am climbing into bed with a stiff drink," "I wanted to lie down with you where the rooftops"

Versions of some of these poems appeared in the chapbooks *She Preferred to Read the Knives* and *How to Live Forever,* both published by Dancing Girl Press.

Sincere thanks to the judges Arda Collins, James Haug, and Dara Wier for selecting my manuscript for the Juniper Prize. Thank you to Courtney Andree, Rachael DeShano, Dawn Potter, and the staff of the University of Massachusetts Press.

Thanks to Kristy Bowen and Dancing Girl Press.

Thanks to Henry Carlile for teaching me clarity, Michele Glazer for teaching me everything else, and the Portland State University writing program and my workshop comrades for keeping the faith.

Thank you to Literary Arts for awarding me an Oregon Literary Fellowship, and thank you to all my colleagues there, past and present.

Thank you to my irrepressible parents who raised me right—
Diane Glassmire and Bill Moore.

Thanks also to my entire family for their support and love—
Jane Moore, Debra Hoxsey, Holly, Tom, Amy, Scott, Melinda, Randy—
and all the nieces and nephews.

Thank you to Laura Kate and Max Denning. I was made to love you.

Thank you to Anna and Kate Ottum for the warm welcome.

Thank you, Cecelia Hagen, first reader,
for your wit and poetry and constant friendship.

Thanks to my poets, all of you for many different reasons—
Carl Adamshick, Heather Brown, Natalie Garyet, Sara Guest, Ada Limón,
Janice MacRae, Liz Mehl, John Morrison, Mary Rechner, Evan P. Schneider,
Naomi Shihab Nye, Ed Skoog, Erika Stevens.

Many thanks to Susan Beekman for her wisdom in many things, including
taking me to see Gary Snyder on the Oregon coast when I was seventeen.

Somewhere in the stars, Tori and Kay, who saw me first.

Thanks to Doc and Sawyer, faithful companions on the journey.

Phil Ottum—again and again, and for all the lifetimes we share, my love.

JUNIPER
JUNIPER PRIZE FOR POETRY

This volume is the forty-sixth recipient of the
Juniper Prize for Poetry, established in 1975 by the
University of Massachusetts Press in collaboration with
the UMass Amherst MFA program for Poets and Writers.
The prize is named in honor of the poet Robert Francis
(1901–1987), who for many years lived in Fort Juniper,
a tiny home of his own construction, in Amherst.